LATER EMPERORS

Greek-Canadian poet Evan Jones [Ευριπίδης Ιωάννου]
lives in Manchester. His first collection, *Nothing Fell Today
But Rain* (Fitzhenry & Whiteside, 2003), was a finalist
for the Governor-General's Literary Award for Poetry. He
co-edited *Modern Canadian Poets* (Carcanet, 2010) and
his British debut, *Paralogues*, was published by Carcanet
in 2012.

Also by Evan Jones

EVAN JONES

Later Emperors

CARCANET

Some of these poems have appeared in *bath magg*, *Berfrois*, *Exile Quarterly*, *Manchester Review*, *PN Review* and *The Walrus*. Thank you to John McAuliffe.

First published in Great Britain in 2020 by
Carcanet
Alliance House, 30 Cross Street
Manchester M2 7AQ
www.carcanet.co.uk

A CIP catalogue record for this book is
available from the British Library.
ISBN 978 1 78410 910 3

Book design by Andrew Latimer
Printed in Great Britain by SRP Ltd, Exeter, Devon

The publisher acknowledges financial
assistance from Arts Council England.

CONTENTS

3   Later Emperors

29   The Further Adventures of Michael Psellos

49   The Journal of Anna Komnene (c. AD 1150)

65   Coda: Plutarch to His Wife

for Marion and Ioanna

LATER EMPERORS

MAXIMIN

When Maximin shouts at the Emperor
Severus, almost in a breath, 'Look at me,
look what I can do,' he is gigantic,
his body is taut but has no purpose
than to flex and recover. Severus
is content. It is his son Geta's birthday.
Look at me, Maximin shouts, look
what I can do. And he never stops,
you know? He will always do.

Eighty years old, thinks the consul Syllanus,
and surrounded by a feeble court, a son
educated in luxury, practically invisible.
Not for their sakes, but the Empire's,
thinks Syllanus. Not for the risk,
but the opportunity. Not for the family
or the progeny, but the Empire. 'Conscript-fathers,'
he begins, the convocation of the Senate
in the temple of Castor, according
to the ancient form of secrecy,
'the two Gordians have been
declared emperors by the consent of Africa.'

GORDIAN II

Gordian the father hears
the voice of Gordian the son
in his head: 'It is nothing. The slip
between valour and death
is nothing.' It is not easy
for the son to say this
to his father, but he says it.

Our lives are like those of Maximus and Balbinus:
the unfortunate soldier and the hopeless noble,
two emperors, alone in the palace, a troop
of assassins approaching, while the city
enjoys the Capitoline games. They are trapped,
more than anything, in their hostility to each other,
unspoken but agreed on. They are unaware
their inner battle is not the problem.

GORDIAN III

His setting out from Rome seems
important. He is seventeen.
The Persians are threatening Antioch.
All around a great army assembles
and marches, his father-in-law
Mistheus beside him. They do not
know any of them what will happen,
but they follow the emperor, for
the first time in years, in person.
They do not know any of them his end
where the Euphrates and Aboras meet,
too unimportant an end to picture now.

When Gordian III asked to remain emperor,
the army booed and hissed.
So he offered to share his power
and the army clanked their spears.
He consented to the rank of Caesar.
But the army refused him.
Could he act then as prefect?
No. They declined outright.
Finally he pleaded for his life.
Philip the Arab, silent till that moment,
considered letting him live.
He thought of Gordian's innocence,
the sympathy the innocent engender,
the riots that sympathy sets in motion,
the half-finished, the order
he was about to give.

DECIUS

All into the marsh at Forum Terebonii,
the despair, the rage and grief,
the heavy Roman armour,
the deep water, the long Goth
spears. The emperor's body
was never found.

GALLUS

On this gold coin, we see Gallus
as a mature man, beard short, crowned,
cuirassed. He is the emperor
who made peace, who gave ground
to Rome's enemies. On the reverse side,
we see Salus, goddess of safety
and health, holding a snake tied
round her staff. It will never quite
reach the food offered in her left hand,
though it knows it can. This the snake
leaves for Gallus, for all that he planned.

AEMILIANUS THE MOOR

There is nothing in the letters
Aemilianus sent to the Senate
of his childhood in North Africa.
Nothing of the goats bleating
or his mother's affection.
He wrote that he would 'assert
the glory of Rome, and deliver
the empire from all barbarians
of the North and of the East';
he declared himself a general,
where the Senate knew the people best.
His reign was short, his ideals never tasked.
He stepped out of his tent one night
woken by what he thought were goats
and his soldiers sacrificed him.

VALERIAN

Yes, yes, the Persian monarch Sapor,
mounting his horse, said to
his allies – they who feared the armies
of Rome – as he steadied his right foot
on Valerian's neck and looked
up through the stars.

GALLIENUS

The young girl carries water to the house,
where once the Emperor Gallienus visited,
passing sheep and goats, the pastures
and fields of her father. She will be
sixteen in the spring and her father
has been dead two years, and her
three brothers, and her grandfather.
The Emperor killed them all, not
by his hand, but his orders, enemies
who were once friends. The slaves
hid her in their chambers,
but the Emperor gave no order
against young girls, so it didn't matter.
Her mother died in childbirth.
She has no memory of that.

It should have been the battle
of Naissus, a Gothic column charging.
It should have been the Senate,
the Republic, a dart, a spear,
even a shield to the head.
These things appeared and he
was firm. But not at the end.
The weakened Empire was weakened
by pestilence. He allowed it to take him.

QUINTILIUS

The cost of his
seventeen-day reign
was low: his death at Aquileia
at the hands of graceless
soldiers or disease or even
the opening of his own veins.
The cost came down to this:
he assumed the purple
and lost his life, Quintilius,
never one to overreact.

AURELIAN

Bring the soldier, Aurelian shouted,
the one who assaulted another's wife,
and fasten him between two trees forced
towards each other. When he's secure,
release the trees. Never mind his name.
There will be no grieving.

ZENOBIA

All that remains of Zenobia's past life
is in ruins: her reign, her studies
of art and literature and history,
the great minds who informed her thinking
when Palmyra took the world stage.
On trial before the Emperor Aurelian,
she lost her nerve and implicated, among others,
the sublime Longinus in crimes
against Rome. He was put to death.
And Zenobia? Sometimes not even
death will leave us sure of an ending.

I imagine the widow of Aurelian
reading Ovid and Virgil in her bed.
She bites an apple, starts a conversation
with her daughter, whose future
she frets over. Let her remain at this peace.
Don't warn her, I say, if you know better,
historian, priest, moralist,
from somewhere along,
don't unwrite what I've written.

TACITUS

Tacitus is too old now. His patience,
his wisdom, could not better
the blood-letting of war. On his death-bed,
the army camped in remote Tyana,
he remembers his garden, his villa,
his morning stroll – life a few months ago –
and in his suffering, he curses
the Senate, the godawful Senate.

The heat in Tarsus is not healing,
comforting heat. The soldiers enjoy it,
but some are sick and can't fight well.
They are used to the mountains. Nonetheless,
Florianus wakes in the morning and knows
he is right to be here, emperor, brother
of Tacitus, supported by the legions.
The serving women fetch
his best attires. He is again for Cydnus.

PROBUS

In the market, Probus
stopped to sample a bit
of cheese, a bit of fish,
and then continued walking
towards the circus, where he'd
ordered transplanted a forest
of five thousand trees filled
with a thousand ostrich,
a thousand stag,
a thousand fallow-deer,
a thousand wild boar.
Tomorrow he would
massacre one hundred
lions and lionesses, two
hundred leopards and three
hundred bears. For today,
cheese and fish were enough
to mask the smell.

Aged, feeble Carus during
the furious night called for his mother,
droned, reeled, balked, barked
at the tent poles and servants.
Feverish now, when young he was a tent
pole, a severe and simple man,
as Gibbon wrote, a soldier,
satisfied with stale bacon
and stone-hard peas. He passed.
We set the imperial pavilion
on fire, suggested it was lightning,
an act of god. Wrong,
I know, though not exactly wrong.

NUMERIAN

Numerian dislikes the food in Ctesiphon.
The light of the sun off the Tigris
burns his eyes, and he confines himself
to the darkness of his tent. This is not
a solution: a solution is the return to Rome,
which the soldiers want and the Persians
will wonder at. He never believed
his father would die, and after he did
Carus still filled the world
with his orders and his fears.
The soldiers can live up to one,
but not the other. Numerian will
not really live up to either.

CARINUS

Why did Carinus believe
his brother's death would elevate him
in Rome or anywhere? He is fiddling
some tribune's young wife
when it comes to him that Numerian's legions,
under Diocletian, are broken and retreating.
Later, in victory, when he can't even think
of her, her husband will remind him that
the Empire is not the emperor.

DIOCLETIAN

Diocletian, having resigned the world,
died where he was born.
For his last nine years he planted
cabbage with his own hands
at Salona. The arts, he said to friends,
often, over dinner, are equally difficult,
but reigning is the most difficult art.
We might like to disagree,
but he lived in an era
when the poets kept silent.

THE FURTHER ADVENTURES OF MICHAEL PSELLOS

As a child, Michael Psellos once fell   off his horse, boarded a caïque
and somewhere downstream slipped   overboard. His parents picked him up.
He never had much luck with girls,   but the ones he loved loved
him back. Between the hills   and the ocean, he made his way
to adulthood and into the retinue   of emperors, a motion of the hand
and a nod of the head brought him   forward. 'He seems to just know
things,' the emperors thought,   pausing at 'things.' One morning,
though, Michael woke up exiled and alone,   his eyes still in his head
(this was a Byzantine worry).   It was only the middle of his long,
late life, and not the end. There were   many days yet for him to exist.

Here is the ladder, here is how   he climbed it: never over-reaching,
even as every step up was an   overreach. The poor man of affairs,
because his hands were cold,   because he winced when the wind hit,
could only go so high. His legs   gave him problems too. The emperor
liked to stand at the top, someone   has to be responsible, and every
now and then kicked so that the whole   thing jolted. That was
his trick. He was the kind to enforce   change. Michael feigned liver
troubles, heartburn, but neither were   reason enough to suggest
early retirement. 'Illness,' the emperor   confirmed, 'closes the valves,
swells an already big head.' Michael   held on, showed the spirit
visible in his body, and how it floated   above his body.

Michael sits on his terrace with   Apollodoros of Damascus.
He has read him so much that   the book dwindles, learning
more about warfare than intended: wall-fighting, the position
of infantry, cavalry skirmishes.   It is early spring, the rain is obvious.
Right, he thinks, coming back to   his work, the book between fingers
and thumb, the feel of it, take   this to the emperor. So that it all rushes
forward at last. So that someone   like himself may question
the role of such a man as himself.   The emperor dislikes questions.
He is in love with his throne,   and only Michael is his friend.

THE FIELD THAT CAUSES NIGHTINGALES

Now the emperor in his clarity   envisions a barren plain
near the City and conceives in it   a fertile field, the concealment
of grasshoppers and nightingales   among blossoming trees.
The emperor's mornings fill up   like this, and he doesn't know,
at this stage, someone to whom   a civilization is entrusted,
he doesn't know, upon whom so many   cares rest, if he can hear
the chirruping and singing. Michael   tries to explain the consequences
of speculation: it isn't the field   that causes nightingales
to sing, even as the sun fuses plant   and insect and animal. He listens
for the emperor's response, but knows: It is me, he means me.

A storm at sea, thunder over   the palace, the emperor is gone.
Another stands to take his place: men support or move
against him. Michael listens   to both arguments
but is remembering the Church   of St George the Martyr.
The emperor had the original   demolished, ordered architects
to plan a loftier basilica high   in the City. Gardens, hanging,
columns on tops of columns,   lawns ornamented with flowers
and fountains – around the base   of one, the bas-relief
of seasons passing. It was,   following the long sigh of construction,
so very moving a place. The emperor   toured his achievement,
but had already lost interest.   All was well and already in the past.

THE INFINITE IS A MUSHROOM

Gradually the stubborn empress died   (she was twenty years older),
and the emperor was seized   by a broken-heartedness.
He went to his advisors, and   'mourning', he said, 'tomb',
he said, 'miracle', he said. Some   consoled him. When he said 'infinite',
Michael understood the words   were as stubborn as the empress.
He thought of Anaxagoras: my mourning is in everything in everything.
The tomb is a bee hive. The miracle   is the royal blood. The infinite
is a mushroom preferred to a peach.   What we offer in our losses
pushes against mortality and can   feel something pushing back.
The emperor liked this. When his   sister died, he barely noticed.

Michael knew who held the   power, but the emperor
liked to remind him, so night   after night he reworked
the occasion of his arrival at court.   He had a soft way of telling
and he spoke of family, the older   sister who'd died young,
the years as clerk and administrator.   Too much. It was not
the coming and going that opened   the emperor's heart. It was not
the eloquence, for the story   slips from the emperor's mind
and needs retelling. The emperor's   heart opened because
Michael knew how to speak and   made speech. The emperor watched
as he turned from person to person,   speaking, everyone, Michael
quietly manoeuvring the room   as the court appears motionless.

There were hundreds of people   in the palace gardens.
The emperor, at one end, listened   to Michael explain philosophy,
the excess and the vanity, the   impoverishment of literature.
They were alone, among hundreds,   except a small girl lay asleep
near the throne, and the emperor   did not wish to wake her.
A gesture by which he hoped to   please the crowd, impress upon it.
Though he pleased himself most.   Michael tapped his walking stick
on the marble, a nervous habit, and   was asked to stop. For years he
has tried to understand this habit, he   did stop, even as the emperor
stood and lifted the girl, sheltering   her from all noise. Michael,
walking stick in hand, stood and   drifted in the direction of the exit.

The empress was in her room,   the emperor upstairs in bed
with his mistress. All agreed this   was a bad idea. A formal oath,
praised by the senators, was   administered and the distress went
this way and that until Michael,   knowing all of this will end,
even if the wind doesn't blow,   elevated the tone of the words:
Little wonder that Trojans and   Akhaians suffer for such
a woman. Well, that Michael,   the senators agreed, consoling
the inconsolable. And out he went,   thinking things all right,
all the signs of acceptance pointing   his way. He retreated home,
sat down to dinner, holding onto   what he had, what he was.
The emperor ordered arrows   shot at those who disagreed.

The emperor's uncle, John,   explained in the morning
that he should not be convicted   among the conspirators.
Not that there were any, but John   bore some secret knowledge.
He was hopeful, Michael thought,   returning to a quiet in his youth,
a dangerous taking away.   John approached the emperor
with the day's requests and   promises. Michael approved,
said that John was a good   man. The emperor agreed.
There once was a man named   John, uncle to the emperor,
though there isn't such a man now.   The body heaves and sighs.
What Michael had to say   couldn't wait until morning.
He woke in the night wondering   if the emperor understood.

Those men, the emperor   ordered, and those men.
The soldiers led fifteen   thousand towards his grace,
knowing, held in the setting   sunlight, their swords' sharpness.
Take the Bulgars' sight,   the emperor ordered.
It was impossible but the   soldiers did it. Then the Bulgars
could see only red through   the smashed windows
of their faces. Opposite, there   was a field of pear trees,
where survivors found their way   to food the Romans didn't want.
Then hounds began to howl,   the music of God among the trees.
The odour of fruit and fighting.   It's not true, Michael tells himself,
a myth of the historians.   He knows the excellence
of the court historians,   their fixed and balanced writing.

They have castrated the rebels.   It comes as a surprise
they were allowed to live,   but the emperor likes to surprise.
People think him glorious,   merciful in finishing these families.
Yet Michael resents the position   he finds himself in.
Not that the emperor was wrong.   Not that the families
wouldn't come back.   God is not unjust.
The outlying members hid   themselves in the Stoudion.
They are only people,   refugees, and the emperor
has today made them   Michael's problem.
He is distressed, the way a bird   in its nest is distressed,
a fox approaching a chick   fallen out. They are hungry.
They are all hungry. Some will   eat. Some will go quiet.

In the old days, Michael,   he and his sister,
playing in the garden.   Their father was a tall man
or so he seemed and   he liked to hear his children
laugh, to feed them   grapes from the vine.
What he remembers   is the sound of his father's voice,
a perfect, whole-hearted   sound unravelled, unprotected.
It remains in Michael's mind   something genuine, maybe
it contains the mystery   of the genuine. He doesn't
remember his own voice,   though it was there, alongside
the usual challenges   and failings of childhood.
In that sense, his was   nothing uncommon. It led here.
He announces his   presence to the emperor.

All glories to dust, yes, like   the library at Alexandria,
the Serapeum. 'But we hold   onto them as ideals,'
argued Michael, 'the glories   lost, the statues fallen.'
The emperor stopped him.   He paced the royal chamber
nightly, the empire buried   under the body of its enemies.
Antioch. Manzikert. Places   that were clues to his ambition,
hidden on the map. His mind,   in this matter, was inflexible.
Michael admired this. 'The helmsman   guides the ship,
the soldier bears arms, the emperor   places trust in God,'
he continued. All cities to rock   and sand. 'I know this!'
shouted the emperor, 'Now   tell me how to hold it all'.
Michael held his fingers to his   lips, after something else.

Then? As slowly as possible,   or nearly as slowly, aware
of the roles being played,   affected manners, though not
at all false, prepared and sorry,   Michael goes back to the beginning.
He has his ideas, a few   conversation pieces, he explains,
set-ups and low-downs. There is   a pattern, a precedence
in the character of emperors,   as they are in time and not eternity.
They believe the opposite to   be the case. They speak it.
'It is less about you than those   who make you. It's not courage
or passion, how quickly you   change horses on the battlefield,
or any fear of bodies of water.   Do you hear the singing?
That's their sorrow. And if you   don't? That's their sorrow.'

The emperor died mysteriously   in his bath. The emperor
was captured and killed at   Manzikert. The emperor was alive,
held to ransom. The emperor   was no more. His brother plotted
a coup. The people rioted. His son   came of age. The empress
took a younger lover. The city   was burning. The plague all-
consuming. The houses and   churches emptied, filled, emptied.
The emperor understood and   said as much. His voice growing
fainter, as the Varangian guard   led him away in chains.

NOT YET NEGLIGIBLE

His voice growing fainter   as the soldiers led him away.
He must be alive somewhere,   heeding an emperor's worries,
warm in front of a fire.   He is not yet negligible.
He will read this and know he   has taken enough of the blame.

THE JOURNAL OF ANNA KOMNENE (C. AD 1150)

ON CHILDHOOD

Yesterday, underneath a pile of old trembling, I found
an assignment from my school days: the topic, 'What Akhilleus
would say seeing the body of Patroklos'. I had tried, looking back,
to position myself between them,

                              the sand and their armour,
the horses. I can see Akhilleus' fingers twitch, he is silent. Patroklos
is grey. The wind coming in off the sea rustles the tent flaps.
I found this years too late. It wasn't well-received.

Let's imagine, at sunset, the tents are pitched on the peak
of the horizon, under the watchman's watchful eye. He
signals his commander who signals his commander
and the table is set,
                              the meal laid out, and the envoys
arrive with their terms and conditions. The gods, as the poet
wrote, do not combat necessity. The wine is good and strong,
the lamb tender, but I'm impatient, celebrating the details.

ON THE LOSS OF HER YOUNGER SIBLINGS
ANDRONIKOS AND EUDOKIA

Lying down, I hear a younger woman laughing, a lark,
the cooing of a dove. She must be pretty, educated,
interested in life, above all, the kind young men notice.
If I disappear into her

the table is set again. We children
sit round our parents at dinner, a feast day. We believe
we are divine, and the sound of our voices overcomes
the forks against the plates, the chewing, the laughter.

ON GRIEF

I read Euripides all day and drink only water.
Tragedy is room temperature, and satisfying,
and bearable. God offers to visit. But I'm too weak.
In a week or two or three
                              the door will open on this cell,
the curtains, then the window. I will eat a light
meal, dress appropriately, and sneak out
into the landscape wearing the mask of, most likely, Elektra.

Of the monody that undoes me as I sing it?
I sing it. I practice from two o'clock in the morning,
not wishing to disturb the birds, but to parallel
through the night their regrets.

                       Who's listening, who's there
in the moonlight and nightwind to hear this? Moonwind.
I don't wish to disturb anyone, but the morning will
arrive and it won't hold still. No sleep till then. Only singing.

Only now they come to me, the works my father returned
to: Isokrates, Pindar, Polemon, Homer, Sappho.
I have my own copies here, presiding over
my reading and spirit

                        as they tormented his, a circus
of ghosts, haunted by muse and lyre, loud enough
to block out the palace. They come to me to argue
in my father's voice. And are nearly as convincing.

ON THE CONVENT MOTHER OF GOD
KECHARITOMENE

My ravaged mother, foresighted, founded this convent
with her power and her shadow, shielding her daughters
under the wing of God. Sealed, separated, alone,
it is almost painful

            to be alive. I've put on weight.
I sleep heavily and wake with my feet and hands
swollen, my legs stiff. I have one responsibility:
the words I write, the words which offer no protection.

Where is it that one is safe? I ask the servants, the nuns.
I dream new words in Homer, read for lines he never wrote,
while somewhere someone else writes them down, the life I thought
was my own. I lie back in bed
                                          because the past contains me,
I sit down to write because I am less real and can perceive
reality for what it is: mortal, misfit. Some of this
happened, some didn't. Where do you want me to begin?

The lords and the ladies of Antioch, many of them were
friends. We were mutually acquainted with literature,
the language, rhetoric, the works of Aristotle,
the dialogues of Plato.
                              I live in an apartment,
alone, surrounded by codices, reading and studying
the statements of men who swore their words were true.
I hope they are, but I know better what they cannot hold.

Swimming close to me, my daughter, Eirene, two of us
in sight of the shore. We shouldn't be here, or wish
we weren't, the water cold, the waves rising,
Eirene and I wading through
                             a lifetime of waves
in the narrowest rivers. And because I never learned
to escape, because the Cumans are always crossing the Ister,
I taught her to welcome them, the unseen, overwhelming waves.

They are exiles of a kind, travelling east city by city, the armies
that they lead unwinding, inarticulate, unmanning
themselves along the way. Some of them mature,
the rest become victims.
                      I'd like to blame them, waving their
swords fearlessly in the direction of our erudition:
but this is so petty, and they aren't arriving here full-
bellied, fists closed, halfway between Christendom and nothing.

But what was my art? I practised in childhood the measure
of the stars, hell-bent as they were on misleading the lot
of our lives. Like this: in the sign of Taurus, a bronze statue
of the Emperor Constantine
                              fell from its plinth, the wind
southwesterly. I knew what to do, then as now. Coming
back to earth, I raised my hand and lowered it sharply
as if first tearing through a spider's web, then through air.

ON JEALOUSY

I sat by the window reading today, half listening
to a magpie's chatter, convinced of my own weaknesses.
Between pages, I heard in the street below someone selling
mastic, incense, saw his cart –

                           two doors strung together.
I looked up. The sun slipped behind the clouds. No one is a
saint who leaves traces of his will, I read in the Scriptures.
Or maybe I wished the thought to be there, preferring it.

CODA: PLUTARCH TO HIS WIFE

Having missed the road to Athens
the messengers arrived at Tanagra where
they told me about our daughter.
I have eaten some, the locals make
decent bread, the weather is temperate and kind.
I walked along the beach a stretch
before beginning, a Corinthian brought wine
as the sun went down and smiled

pouring it into my bowl with a lively
eagerness that took me back
to a moment in Rome years ago
sitting with a friend when a calmness
overcame me. I was surprised then
as I am now, an unsuitable and unhelpful
sensation that I find myself welcoming
huddled over the resolve of your letter.

Listening, my amanuensis, Petrus,
writes as I drink. Scratch that, start again.
Yes, he will. He pens the words but ignores them.
I try to treat him well. My fellow Greek is educated,
speaks four languages, holds onto
his family – family – and travels wherever
I go: Leptis Magna to Magna Graecia.
He will inherit when I die,

receiving a home and garden, fields,
the space to make his own
of what he will and can. We have dined
at the same table, talked and prayed.
He knows the map of the world
and has seen what I have seen these
past few years. A remarkable man
who in any circumstances might ask,

questioning my words, who was
the emperor then? How many members
of the Areopagus? In what way was Sabinus
the Gaul involved? I encourage his
inquisitiveness though tonight he
remains silent and does not look up
as I say these things. His mathematics
are strong, I formulated once, oh, I am

losing track of my thoughts, the life
of Petrus, which you know, wise woman
and wife, the closeness of two people
travelling, the costs of travel
beyond fortune, the distance from home
and family. I can see not too far off
the outline of our closeness
and the ways in which that fades,

unfurling as so gently in the wind one's
eyes are closed and soon enough
another leaves and what little happiness
there was separates and weighs
on the living rest. Life is made thin
and there is so much in the grave past
and graver future. Musicians, songs of the sea
interrupt the ache of helplessness:

knowing the Corinthian can offer this
I want it, though his timeliness is
inappropriate within my loss, your loss,
the small joys and eases of the heart.
The people here are nice, what is more
they seem to recognise in me someone
who will welcome the hours stolen away
through their efforts, because I am trying,

trying to see through this. They do not,
the musicians I mean, they do not come
here from Rome or Athens. Tanagra
is a provincial town and the locals are local
such that they claim to have cousins
as far as Sicily. The Corinthian really isn't,
born there but with less title from
that city than I might have,

overhearing a conversation between friends,
listening in to pick up their accent
and delivery, a sort of boorish teenager
who seeks to set himself up with a trade
and identity but lacking in either, no
apprenticeship, no skills but willpower
pushing him forward. I understand
the appeal but not the urgency.

Pretending is a formality. Better the voice,
I suppose, a reward for accomplishment,
and not the accomplishment itself. From where
is the reward? What is accomplished?
I've been asking and hear no answers.
That is not the way to address the
question, I know, yet an unfoundedness
is acceptable in inquiry and understanding.

Learning from imperfect teachers,
children fill the hollow until they might themselves
entertain to read and learn becoming
imperfect in their own right. Then exile
or death, one or the other, the former puts off
the latter, but the body is laid to rest, always.
The child, our child, in the ground.
You and I have seen this many times.

Asking whether we might reach perfection
is problematic. Only the gods are perfect
and in our seeking their heights
we fail, universally, because every ambition
is godliness on Earth. Only poets
ever achieve this and they recognise
the cost. Euripides, Aeschylus.
My knowledge of the habits of men,

mediating between the few and the fewer,
started here, as not everyone is after
their lives in this fashion. And that is
where I think of Timoxena, the pleasure
I took in her presence. This was a mistake,
I realise, unreliable child that she was,
late for lunch and dinner, dancing,
preoccupied, scratches over her legs,

studying unfinished, never sleeping, never
tired, not always pleasant, to be fair,
but my attachment to her a solid,
visible thread, as family and home become
wound together. And unwound. My grief
has only it limits, the death of a daughter
amounting to the pain already
present from fear of such a death.

Imagining we can be ready for an event
when it happens never works, never has.
Reality serves to obliterate itself and us
alongside. I will hold myself in order for this.
The Corinthian and Petrus offered sympathies,
of course, they are generous men, something
one can hear in their voices, solitary
amid the din, a rare find, an ability,

confiding their own memories and worries,
but I feel alone for the moment,
the ghosts of ancestors departed
and freeing me to take on the future.
That would be a change, wouldn't it?
I have always lived in the past, an insult
I once thought, where I sought the benefit
of going over what others would ignore,

quickening their pace beyond what love
obliges that I recover. And our daughter.
The wine is strong and good, it brings
the space for these words to retire with grace.
Timoxena, I will always love you, daughter
and wife of the same name, our family
will thrive, it always has, for thriving is
common, easy as earning money.

Attending to old family, new family, children
and parents, we have known them and lost,
the feelings unfocused but pure
in their intentions. When my father
turned the page and couldn't remember
the house he lived in, we cared as best
we could, and the daughters and sons, born
and unborn, knew they were loved.

Deliberating and choosing not this life
but the next, is fine, really, just fine.
I am cold. The wine. Petrus looks worried.
The letter begun in haste is always mishandled.
The concerns and the revelations
of immortality and not mortality are where
our hopes must remain. Petrus: I will start again.
Having missed the road to Athens…

Browning to Ruskin: 'Do you think poetry was ever generally understood – or can be? Is the business of it to tell people what they know already, as they know it, and so precisely that they shall be able to cry out – *'Here you should supply* this – that, *you evidently pass over, and I'll help you from my own stock'?* It is all teaching, on the contrary, and the people hate to be taught'.